INA PAARMAN

WHAT'S ON THE
BRAAI?

TRIED & TESTED ✓

PUBLISHED BY PAARMAN FOODS

www.paarman.co.za

GRIDDLE COOKED BUTTERFLIED LEG OF LAMB

CONTENTS

Published by Paarman Foods
First published 2005. Revised in 2007

TEXT	Ina Paarman
PHOTOGRAPHY	Nikki Boss
PRODUCTION & DESIGN	Haumann Smal Design Studio
FOOD PREPARATION & STYLING	Ina Paarman Janet Hacking Elizabeth Copeland
COORDINATION	Lilo Keeson
PRINTED & BOUND BY	Hansa Reproprint
DISTRIBUTED BY	Paarman Foods PO Box 316 Constantia 7848

ISBN 0-620-33641-2

FRESH WATERMELON IN AN ICE BOWL

BEGINNINGS
& ENDINGS

Delicious as a starter or as part of an outdoor fish buffet.

CHEESY CRUMBED MUSSELS

SERVES 4

1 kg fresh or 500 g frozen black mussels on the half shell
1 x 200 ml Ina Paarman's Ready to Serve Cheese Sauce
2-3 T (30-45 ml) olive oil
4 cloves of crushed garlic
1 cup (250 ml) fresh white breadcrumbs
Ina Paarman's Lemon and Black Pepper Seasoning
finely snipped chives or chopped parsley to garnish

If using fresh mussels, steam them open in their own juices in a large saucepan with a tight fitting lid. Shake the pan over high heat for 5 minutes. Discard any unopened mussels. Remove the top shell-half. No need to steam if using frozen mussels – just thaw. Snip a small hole in the top corner of the Cheese Sauce doypack and squeeze generously over each mussel. Place in a single layer in an oven pan.

Sauté the garlic in the oil for a few seconds and then add the crumbs to the pan, season and toss until lightly coated and just beginning to turn golden. Cover the mussels with the crumbs.* Flash the mussels under a hot grill for a few minutes or warm them on the braai. Garnish with chives or parsley.

CHEF'S TIP
* Can be prepared in advance to this point.

BEST GUACAMOLE

SERVES 6

3 large avocados
3 cloves of crushed garlic
1¹/₂ t (7,5 ml) Ina Paarman's Chilli and
   Garlic Seasoning
juice of half a lime or lemon
1-2 packets (150-300 g) Cheese Nacho
   Chips

*I really recommend making this
at the last minute – you can
always rope in a guest to help.
If you have to prepare beforehand,
put the pip back into the mixture
as it prevents browning. Remove
the pip just before serving.*

Cube the avocados and then roughly crush
them with a wire whisk or fork in a small mixing
bowl. Add the garlic, seasoning and lime juice.
Mix lightly – don't pulverize too much. Serve
immediately with Cheese Nacho Chips.

CHEF'S TIP

Getting the best out of avocados
*Select avocados with dull, matt-looking skins.
Pear-shaped avocados should have fat necks and
feel heavy for their size when weighed in your
hand. To speed up ripening, wrap avocados up in
newspaper with a ripe apple or banana and store
in a dark cupboard. The fruit releases ethylene
gas which accelerates the ripening process of the
avocados considerably.*

BABY MARROW AND SALMON ROLLS

MAKES 24-30

6 baby marrows
olive oil
Ina Paarman's Lemon and Black Pepper
    Seasoning
1 x 250 g tub salmon flavoured cream
    cheese
100-200 g peppered salmon trout, or
    peppered mackerel
fresh dill, chives or fennel
toothpicks

Top and tail the marrows. Cut them
lengthways into 2-3 mm thick strips.
Brush the strips with olive oil on both
sides and season.

Grill on a hot, ribbed griddle pan. Leave
to cool. Roll strips around your finger
and secure with a toothpick.

Pipe or spoon a little cream cheese into
each roll and then stand a piece of
flaked salmon in the centre. Garnish
with a sprig of fresh herbs.

*These mini snacks
look lovely, although
they take a little
more effort.*

8

FETA SPREAD WITH SUN-DRIED TOMATOES

SERVES 12

1 x 225 g tub feta cheese, drained
half a pack of Ina Paarman's Sun-dried
    Tomato Quarters in olive oil
    vinaigrette, drained
2 T (30 ml) olive oil
2 t (10 ml) Ina Paarman's Chilli and Garlic
    Seasoning
1 x 250 g tub smooth cottage cheese
1 cup (250 ml) plain Greek style yoghurt
half a punnet of watercress (optional)

Roughly cube the feta and drain the
sun-dried tomatoes. Place all the
ingredients except watercress in a
food processor and blend until smooth. Serve
at room temperature with toasted
French bread slices, crostini or
crackers. Serve and garnish with
watercress.

CHEF'S TIP
*This recipe can be made a few days in
advance and kept in the fridge. Do not
freeze.*

Everybody loves this!

9

CHEESY POLENTA TARTLETS WITH PESTO AND FRESH TOMATOES

MAKES 36 TARTLETS

4 cups (1 litre) water
3 T (45 ml) Ina Paarman's Chicken Stock
    Powder
1 heaped cup (180 g) coarse yellow
    polenta (mieliemeal)
3 T (45 ml) butter
1/2 cup (125 ml) grated pecorino cheese

TOPPING
1 x 125 g Ina Paarman's Basil Pesto
36 fresh basil leaves (smallish ones)
18 baby tomatoes, halved

Bring the water to the boil and add the chicken stock powder. Add the polenta in a thin stream to the stock while whisking with a wire whisk.

Cook slowly with the lid on for 20 minutes stirring occasionally. Stir in the butter and cheese. Oil three mini-muffin pans and fill the hollows with the polenta mixture.

Smooth the tops over neatly with a palatte knife or scraper. Leave to stand overnight or for a couple of hours to firm at room temperature.

Remove the tartlets from the pan. Spread each one with basil pesto. Top with a fresh basil leaf and half a baby tomato.

SPICED NUTS

MAKES 2 CUPS

1 egg white
2 cups (200 g) assorted unsalted, raw
    nuts (such as walnuts, pecans,
    almonds or macadamias)
2 t (10 ml) Ina Paarman's Chilli and Garlic
    Seasoning
1½ t (7,5 ml) sugar

Preheat the oven to 180°C.

Line a large baking sheet with baking paper and brush with oil. In a large bowl, whisk egg white until foamy. Add nuts, seasoning and sugar. Toss to coat evenly. Spread nuts in a single layer on the baking sheet. Bake, stirring once or twice, for about 10 minutes until nuts are crisp and aromatic. Allow to cool.

Serve slightly warm or at room temperature. Stores well in an airtight container for up to a week. Can be re-crisped in the oven for 3 minutes.

There are all kinds of tricky recipes for glazed nuts that involve deep-frying. We've come up with a simple way to make them in the oven. The secret is the egg white, which helps the seasoning and sugar to adhere and adds an attractive glazed finish. Serve as a cocktail, snack or tossed into salads.

Prepare the glaze well in advance and keep it in the fridge. Delicious over summer berries and seasonal fruits. Serve in individual martini shaped glasses or in a beautiful goblet shaped glass bowl.

PEACHES AND BERRIES WITH RED WINE GLAZE

SERVES 6

RED WINE GLAZE
3/4 cup (187 ml) sugar
1 cup (250 ml) red wine
3 cloves
1/4 t (1 ml) black pepper (don't omit, it
    lends an excellent flavour)
2 t (10 ml) grated lemon peel
1 T (15 ml) balsamic vinegar
Boil the sauce ingredients in an open saucepan for about 10 minutes until syrupy and aromatic. Cool and reserve until needed.

6 ripe nectarines or peaches, sliced
100-150 g raspberries, blueberries, etc

Pour a tablespoon of glaze into each glass. Add peaches and berries (the peaches are at their best if sliced just before serving). Drizzle wine glaze over the fruit and serve with Greek yoghurt or whipped cream.

CHEF'S TIP
Substitute for wine: red grape juice, but reduce sugar to 2/3 cup (160 ml).

COCONUT CHEESECAKE WITH STRAWBERRIES

SERVES 6-8

FILLING
3/4 cup (187 ml) coconut milk (freeze the rest for another dish)
1 x 250 g Ina Paarman's Lemon Cheesecake Mix
1/2 cup (125 ml) puréed fresh strawberries
1 cup (250 ml) fresh whipping cream

CRUST
3 T (45 ml) butter, melted
11 tennis biscuits, crushed

PREPARING THE PAN *Use a loose-bottom 20 cm diameter cake tin or springform pan. Line only the base with a neat circle of greaseproof or baking paper.*

Measure the coconut milk into a medium size mixing bowl. Sprinkle the cheesecake mix over the coconut milk and beat until well blended. Cover with clingfilm and leave in the fridge. Chop about 1 cup of fresh strawberries in a blender or food processor to make 1/2 cup of purée. In a smaller mixing bowl whip the cream until stiff. Remove the cheesecake mixture from the fridge. Using the same beaters, whip the mixture for 1 minute until smooth. Add the strawberry purée. Gently fold the whipped cream into the cheesecake mixture using a spatula or metal spoon and stir until evenly blended. Pour the cheesecake mixture into the prepared pan. Melt the butter, add the biscuit crumbs and mix together with a fork. Sprinkle over the cheesecake mixture in pan. Press crumbs down and smooth gently with the back of a spoon. Cover and set in the fridge overnight.

TO SERVE *Loosen the cake gently all round with a thin bladed knife dipped into boiling water and turn upside down on a cake stand.*

GARNISH
250 g fresh strawberries
2-3 T (30-45 ml) strawberry or apricot jam
Thinly slice the hulled strawberries as illustrated. Arrange over the cake. Brush with warmed jam thinned down with a teaspoon or two of water if necessary.

VARIATION: GRANADILLA CHEESECAKE WITH KIWI
Use 1/2 cup (125 ml) of fresh granadilla pulp in the cake instead of strawberry purée and serve slices with kiwi fruit and a granadilla half on the side.

13

An absolute classic! Never fails to get rave reviews.

TRIFLE DELUXE

SERVES 12-14

1 ready made swiss roll, or 6 mini swiss rolls
1/2 cup (125 ml) sherry, port or sweet dessert wine
1/2 cup (125 ml) glacé cherries, halved
4 preserved green figs, roughly chopped
4 nuggets preserved ginger, finely sliced
1/2 cup (125 ml) flaked almonds, lightly toasted in a dry pan
4 cups (1 litre) good quality ready made custard
1/2 cup (125 ml) cream
extra whole cherries, nuts and sliced preserved figs

Slice the swiss roll. Place 1/3 of swiss roll slices in a large glass bowl. Mix the cherries, figs, ginger and almonds together. Sprinkle with 1/3 of sherry. Sprinkle with 1/3 of fruits and nuts. Coat with 1/3 of custard. Repeat layers twice more. Cover top with half-whipped cream. Decorate with whole cherries, nuts and sliced figs. Chill for at least 3 hours.

VARIATION
Replace the ginger with 4 rings of crystallized pineapple, finely sliced.

CHEF'S TIP
Preserved figs are not always available. We have often substituted them with crystallized figs for the same delicious flavour.

14

CARAMEL TOPPED NUTTY CHOCOLATE CHIP BROWNIES

MAKES 16 SQUARES

2 extra large eggs
1/4 cup (60 ml) melted butter
1/2 cup (125 ml) canola or sunflower oil
1/2 cup (125 ml) full cream milk
1 x 550 g Ina Paarman's Chocolate
    Brownie Mix
1/4 cup (60 ml) chopped pecan nuts

FUDGE TOPPING

100 g dark eating chocolate
1/2 large tin boiled sweetened condensed
    milk (see *Chef's Tip*)
extra pecan nut halves to garnish

Delight your guests with this decadent bake – moist, chewy chocolate brownies topped with caramel and pecan nuts.

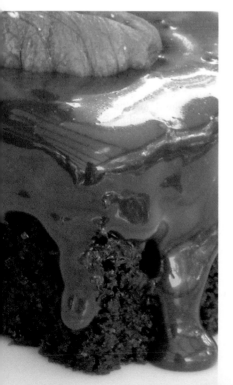

Preheat oven to 180°C.

Adjust oven rack to middle position. Prepare a pan (20 cm x 20 cm square or 20 cm x 30 cm rectangular) – see illustrated instructions on Chocolate Brownie Mix box. Beat eggs, melted butter and oil for 2 minutes on high speed until well blended. Add milk and beat for 1 minute on medium speed. Add Brownie Mixture, chocolate chips (included with Brownie Mix) and nuts and fold in carefully with a spatula. Blend until just combined – do not beat. Mixing by hand gives the best results. Scrape mixture into the prepared pan.

Bake on middle shelf for 35 - 40 minutes. Brownies are done when a thin bladed knife inserted in the centre comes out clean or cake pulls away slightly from the sides of the pan. Leave to cool down completely. Cut into 16 squares.

Melt the dark eating chocolate in a glass mixing bowl over boiling water and mix it in with the caramel. Spread the chocolate-caramel over the pre-cut brownies when cooled. Pull the squares apart while the topping is still a bit soft to get a yummy rundown effect. Garnish each square with half a pecan nut.

CHEF'S TIP

How to boil condensed milk for fudge topping

Boil one tin (397 g) of sweetened full cream condensed milk slowly for 45 minutes in a pot with enough water to cover the tin. Cool in a bowl of cold water before you open the can as the hot caramel may spurt up and burn you. The other half of the caramel will keep well if refrigerated in a sealed container.

FRESH WATERMELON IN AN ICE BOWL

ICE BOWL

An ice bowl makes an impressive serving dish for fresh fruit, ice cream or sorbet. Make the bowl well in advance and store it in the freezer. We used bougainvillea flowers set in the ice because of the wonderful colour match with watermelon.

Select two bowls, one about 5 cm smaller than the other. Choose plastic or stainless steel bowls, as we found that a glass bowl can shatter when frozen. Put ice cubes in the bottom of the larger bowl and place the smaller bowl on top. Tape the bowls at intervals at the edges to keep them an even distance apart. Place flowers between the bowls and pour in cold water to fill the gap.

Freeze the bowls. Use a skewer to push the flowers down between the bowls if they float during freezing. To release the ice bowl, remove the tape and pour a little hot water into the small bowl and stand the bottom bowl in hot water. As soon as the ice bowl is released place it in the freezer, on a double layer of greaseproof paper, until you are ready to use it.

Chill a ripe watermelon until serving time. Split open and cut the flesh into wedges. Pile into the prepared ice bowl and serve with fresh berries.

16

FRESH LEMONADE

MAKES ABOUT 2 LITRES OF SYRUP
- KEEP REFRIGERATED

LEMON SYRUP CONCENTRATE

Juice and grated zest of 4 juicy lemons
5 cups (1 kg) white sugar
2 T (30 g) citric acid
1 T (15 g) tartaric acid
5 cups (1,25 litres) boiling water

First grate off the outer skin of the
lemons on the fine side of a grater or
use a microplane. Place the lemon juice
and zest in a large saucepan. Add the
sugar, citric acid and tartaric acid. Pour
the boiling water over and stir to
dissolve the sugar. Just bring to the
boil and remove from the heat
immediately. Cool, then pour into clean
bottles and refrigerate until needed.
Makes around 2 litres and keeps for a
month refrigerated.

TO MIX A JUG OF LEMONADE
SERVES 6

1 cup lemon syrup
1 tray of ice cubes
1 lemon cut into half slices
1 litre of soda or sparkling water
Fresh mint (optional)

Mix everything in a glass jug. Stir before
pouring.

VARIATION:
Add a tot of gin or vodka to each glass
before topping up with lemonade mixture.

CHEF'S TIP

GET MORE JUICE OUT OF LEMONS
Prick the lemons and microwave them for
30 seconds on high.

This is a wonderful drink to
have on tap during the hot
summer months.

SKEWERED LAMB CHOPS

HOTTING UP

It is best to buy the pre-tenderised frozen calamari steaks. Thaw them out covered with a little buttermilk or plain yoghurt – this assists in further tenderizing and whitening the calamari.

CAJUN-STYLE CALAMARI STEAK STRIPS IN TORTILLA CONES

SERVES 6

6 frozen calamari steaks
   (about 150-200 g each)

CAJUN MIX

3 t (15 ml) Ina Paarman's Cajun Spice
2 t (10 ml) flour
olive oil
2 limes or lemons
6 soft flour tortillas (cut in half)
1 punnet rocket leaves

Defrost the steaks as suggested above and pat them dry with paper towels. Mix the Cajun Spice and flour together. Rub it into the steaks. Brush steaks generously with olive oil.

Cook for about 5 minutes on each side on a very hot griddle pan or braai grid until well marked on both sides. Place on a wooden chopping board and with a very sharp knife, slice the steaks into $1/2$ cm wide strips. Squeeze a little lime or lemon juice over. Warm the tortillas according to packet instructions. Roll tortilla halves into cone shapes and stuff with rocket and strips of cooked calamari. Serve with lime wedges.

CHEF'S TIP
Instead of tortillas use pancakes cut in half, or stuff into halved pita breads.

20

CRAYFISH AND SALMON STEAKS OVER THE COALS

SERVES 4 AS PART OF A FISH BUFFET

2 whole crayfish or 4 tails
2-4 salmon steaks
Ina Paarman's Lemon and Black Pepper
Seasoning or Chilli and Garlic
Seasoning
olive oil

SPLITTING CRAYFISH

1. Grip back firmly. Pierce sharply at central point where head meets body. Halve head.

2. Split in half lengthways. Remove the vein. Rinse under cold running water.

Season the crayfish halves and salmon steaks with the Seasoning of your choice. Brush with a generous amount of olive oil.

Prepare a medium/hot fire. Make sure that your braai grid is spotlessly clean. Rub the grid with the cut side of a raw onion or a little oil to prevent food from sticking to it. Place the crayfish, meaty side down, and cook for 3-5 minutes. When nicely marked, turn the tails over and cook on the shell side for about 7 minutes. Cook the salmon steaks for the same length of time.

Serve as is – a sauce is really not needed, but pickled Japanese ginger is an excellent accompaniment!

With the exorbitant price of crayfish, one almost feels guilty to indulge in this delicacy. All the more reason to make sure you use the best possible preparation and cooking techniques. Keeping it simple is the best policy.

BUTTERFLIED PRAWNS

16-20 large black tiger prawns (± 1 kg)

Ina Paarman's Chilli and
    Garlic Seasoning
1 cup (250 ml) Ina Paarman's
    Lemon Marinade
kebab sticks

If frozen, leave the prawns in a sink half filled with cold tap water until beginning to thaw. Separate from each other and remove the heads. Cut through the hard shell, along the backs, with a pair of kitchen scissors and then slice each prawn almost completely through the flesh, with a sharp knife, to butterfly them open. Remove the black vein and rinse in clean water.

Skewer the prawns on wooden kebab sticks to keep them flat. Season lightly with Chilli & Garlic Seasoning and brush both sides with Marinade. Leave covered in the fridge, with an ice brick on top, until ready to cook.

Prepare a hot griddle pan or braai fire and cook the prawns, meaty side down, until well marked. Turn over and cook on the shell side for 3 minutes.

CHEF'S TIP
Kebab Sticks are made out of bamboo and are thinner and and more fragile than sosatie sticks. Kebab sticks are best suited to smaller portions such as prawns, cubes of fish and vegetables.

Sosatie Sticks are sturdy wooden sticks best suited to larger cuts of meat and chicken.

GRIDDLE PAN FISH OVER THE COALS

SERVES 6

1 whole fish ± 2-2,5 kg carefully selected and cleaned (see *Chef's Tip* below)
Ina Paarman's Fish Spice
1 cup (250 ml) Ina Paarman's Lemon Marinade
fresh origanum, fennel or garlic chives

Prepare a medium hot fire and rub a ribbed iron griddle pan with the cut side of half an onion. This prevents the fish from sticking to the pan.

Season the fleshy side of the fish with Fish Spice, cover the fish, put a few ice bricks on top and refrigerate for 30 minutes to firm the flesh.

Brush the fish generously on the fleshy side with Lemon Marinade. Place, fleshy side down, on the preheated griddle pan over the fire. Baste the skin side with Marinade. Check the fleshy side and as soon as it has browned and is deeply marked with well defined grid marks, it must be turned using two large flat lifters. The fish is not turned again – complete cooking with the skin side down to prevent any loss of delicious juices. Baste generously with the Lemon Marinade on the fleshy side. Test for doneness by pulling the flesh apart at the thickest part of the fish with a fork. As soon as the flesh is white and flaky and no longer opaque and jellyish, the fish is done.

Carefully lift the fish onto a wooden cutting board for serving. Garnish with fresh herbs. Delicious with grilled lemon slices, grilled flat breads (see page 62) and a fresh salad dressed with our Herb or Honey Mustard dressing.

Buy fish that is fresh and in season. Fish frozen at sea and freshly defrosted (once only!) is also acceptable. During the summer months Cape salmon, kabeljou, red roman, yellowtail and steenbras are freely available. During the winter months look out for galjoen and snoek. Hake is in season all year round.

CHEF'S TIP

SELECTION *Select a fish with clear bulbous eyes. Bloodshot sunken eyes are a bad sign in both fish and people! The flesh must have a healthy pinkish hue – grey flesh indicates fish that is old and has been frozen and defrosted more than once.*
CLEANING *Ask the fishmonger to scale and "vlek" the fish for you. "Vlekking" means the belly cavity is slit open from head to tail, the spine is filleted out, but the head and tail remain intact.*

23

FISH IN NEWSPAPER

SERVES 6-8

1 whole fish (about 2,5 kg) Cape salmon,
    kabeljou (cob) or stockfish (hake)
Ina Paarman's Lemon and Black Pepper
    Seasoning
1 t (5 ml) sugar
2 T (30 ml) Ina Paarman's Tomato Pesto
4 T (60 ml) butter, softened
2 T (30 ml) lemon juice
4-6 cloves of crushed garlic
3 ripe red tomatoes, sliced
Ina Paarman's Garlic and Herb Seasoning
fresh basil, origanum or marjoram
1 medium onion, sliced and loosened
    into rings

Scale the fish first, "vlek" it open along the belly and remove the backbone. Leave the head and tail intact. Season the fish with Lemon and Black Pepper seasoning and sugar on the inside. Mix the tomato pesto, butter, lemon juice and garlic together. Spread a generous layer over the one side of the fish. Add the tomato slices and season with Garlic and Herb seasoning. Add the fresh herbs and onion rings.

Fold the fish to cover the filling. Place the whole fish on a large sheet of greaseproof or baking paper and wrap it up. Now re-wrap the fish in 5 sheets of newspaper and tie with string. Wet the paper thoroughly with cold tap water. Make a hollow in the coals of the braai fire and nest the fish amongst the warm coals. Also cover the fish with a few coals. Bake slowly. Allow 45-60 minutes for a 2,5 kg kabeljou. When the fish is done, the outer layers of the newspaper will be scorched.

Slide two sturdy lifters under the fish and carefully remove from the coals. Place on a clean sheet of newspaper and cut open the charred newspaper. You will find that the skin comes away easily from the tender, aromatic fish as you pull away the greaseproof paper.

Delicious served with hot garlic bread, a crisp green salad dressed with our Lite Greek dressing or Lemon Vinaigrette.

CHEF'S TIP
If cooking the fish on a kettle braai, it is not necessary to bury it amongst the coals. Cook on top of the grid with the lid closed.

Fish wrapped in wet newspaper and cooked amongst coals, or in a pizza oven is a delicacy to rave about.

RICE SALAD WITH SEAFOOD

SERVES 6 GENEROUSLY

1¼ cups (250 g) of long grain rice
3 cups (750 ml) water
2 T (30 ml) Ina Paarman's Vegetable Stock
    Powder
1 punnet (200 g) young or baby spinach
    leaves
olive oil
1 red bell pepper
1 yellow bell pepper
Ina Paarman's Green Onion Seasoning
500 g raw, shelled prawns (frozen)
1 t (5 ml) Ina Paarman's Chilli & Garlic
    Seasoning
500 g raw mussels or calamari rings
black pepper
3 whole lemons, cut away all the skin
    and white pith and cut out the lemon
    segments
½ cup (125 ml) caper berries
200 g baby rosa or cherry tomatoes,
    halved
½ cup (125 ml) Ina Paarman's Greek
    Lemon Vinaigrette
fresh basil leaves

A delicious main course salad with intense flavours full of surprises.

Place the rice, water and Stock Powder in a saucepan and cook for 15 minutes until the rice is tender. Add the spinach and 3 T of olive oil. Toss gently until the spinach wilts. Taste for seasoning. Dish into a large mixing bowl.

Blacken the bell pepper over a gas flame or under a grill and put into a covered bowl or plastic bag to 'sweat' for 10 minutes. Remove the skin and pips. Slice into thin strips. Season with Green Onion Seasoning. Fork into the rice. Bring 2 cups of water to the boil in a medium size saucepan. Add all the prawns (still frozen). When they come to the boil, cook them over a gentle heat for 1 minute only. Strain in a colander. Return prawns to the saucepan and toss with 2 T olive oil and Chilli & Garlic Seasoning. Fork into the rice mixture.

Place the mussels in the same saucepan. Cover with a lid (don't add any liquid) and shake over high heat until the mussels open. Season with black pepper and spoon over the rice mixture.

TO ASSEMBLE THE SALAD

Toss the lemon segments, capers and halved baby tomatoes (seasoned with Green Onion Seasoning) with the rice. Dish the salad mixture into a serving platter. Pour the dressing over the salad just before serving. Garnish with fresh basil.

VARIATION: *If mussels are unavailable, briefly stir-fry 500 g baby calamari tubes in a little olive oil and use them.*

PRAWN AND CHICKEN COMBO WITH PERI-PERI PREGO SAUCE

SERVES 4

Expensive, but absolutely delicious. Ideal if you have a wok pan suitable for stir-frying on the braai.

1 kg tiger prawns in the shells with heads on
Ina Paarman's Fish Spice
1 t (5 ml) Ina Paarman's Lemon & Black
    Pepper Seasoning
1 T (15 ml) flour
1 x 400 g chicken mini fillets
$1/4$ cup (60 ml) olive or canola oil
1 x 200 ml Ina Paarman's Peri-Peri Coat
    & Cook Sauce or Lemon Marinade
$1/2$ - $3/4$ cup (180 ml) fresh cream
4 cloves of garlic, finely sliced and chopped
$1/4$ cup (60 ml) chopped parsley
grated skin of one lemon

Defrost the prawns in lukewarm tap water. Pull off the heads and slash open along the backs, remove the black vein that runs along the back. Spread each prawn open with a toothpick. Pack prepared prawns out on a platter and season the meaty side quite generously with Fish Spice. Add oil to the wok. Swipe the meaty side of the prawns through the oil and lay the prawns down on the sides of the wok. Cook until nicely browned and then turn. Remove the prawns, keep on one side - no need to cover or keep warm. Dip and turn chicken mini fillets in a mixture of Lemon & Black Pepper and flour.

Cook the strips of chicken in exactly the same way as the prawns. Add the Peri-Peri Sauce or Lemon Marinade and cream to the chicken in the wok, bring to the boil, add the prawns and just heat through. Mix the sliced garlic, parsley and lemon rind and sprinkle over the dish. Serve immediately with a large bowl of savoury rice and a tossed salad dressed with our Caesar Dressing.

STICKY CHICKEN WINGS

SERVES 4

18 - 24 chicken wings
1 t (5 ml) Ina Paarman's Chicken Spice
1 cup (250 ml) Ina Paarman's
Sticky Marinade

Preheat oven to 180 °C. Snip off the hard feathery pointed end of each wing with a pair of kitchen scissors. Toss the wings with Chicken Spice and the Sticky Marinade. Dish into an ovenproof dish best side up. Bake uncovered for about an hour until crispy and brown or cook slowly on the braai while turning and basting.

Excellent with flash-fried cherry tomatoes, garlic bread and a green salad.

Allow at least four wings per person - they are seriously addictive!

TOMATO AND MUSHROOM PIZZA

SERVES 4

2 large plain pre-cooked pizza bases
1 x 125 g Ina Paarman's Sun-dried
  Tomato Pesto
1 punnet (250 g) sliced button
  mushrooms
Ina Paarman's Garlic Pepper Seasoning
150 g mozzarella or smoked cheese,
  grated
1 small punnet (250 g) baby tomatoes,
  cut in half lengthways
10 black olives, pipped and sliced
olive oil
Ina Paarman's Italian Cheese Sprinkle
fresh origanum or basil

Prepare a low fire and place a large griddle pan or baking sheet on the grid to prevent the pizza from burning. Spread pizza bases with pesto and arrange sliced mushrooms on top. Season with Garlic Pepper seasoning. Sprinkle with cheese and top with halved tomatoes and olives. Drizzle with olive oil and bake with the lid of the braai closed for about 10-12 minutes until heated through.

Sprinkle with Italian Cheese sprinkle and fresh herbs after baking and serve straight away.

CHEF'S TIP
A wood fired pizza oven is the perfect cooking vessel.

VARIATION
Use our Basil Pesto instead of Tomato Pesto.

BEER CAN CHICKEN

SERVES 4-5

1 large free range fresh chicken
1 t (5 ml) Ina Paarman's Chicken Stock
   Powder
1 t (5 ml) Ina Paarman's Braai and Grill
   Seasoning
1/2 t (2,5 ml) Garlic and Herb Seasoning
1 x 340 ml can of beer

*This unusual braai-steam method gives
excellent results. The beer creates moisture
and flavour in the cavity while the chicken
is cooking, keeping the meat beautifully
juicy. The steam also helps the seasonings
to penetrate throughout the meat.*

*If time permits, soak the bird beforehand
for 1 hour in a brine solution. It gives
an even juicier, more succulent result
(see below).*

BRINE SOLUTION

1/4 cup (60 ml) coarse salt (or if using
   table salt reduce by 2 T (30 ml)
1/4 cup (60 ml) brown or yellow sugar
1 litre cold tap water
1/4 cup (60 ml) lemon juice

Mix all the ingredients together to
dissolve. Pour the brine mixture into a
resealable plastic bag. Add the chicken.
Roll the bag up tight against the chicken
so it is covered by the brine. Secure
with a peg or clip. Leave at room
temperature for 1 hour. (Minimum
brining time is 30 minutes and
maximum 6 hours). Remove the
chicken from the brine and pat dry.

Mix the stock powder and seasonings together
and sprinkle half of the mixture inside the
chicken's cavity. Rub the rest into the skin.
Drink a 1/4 of the can of beer and then remove
the top completely with a can opener. Soak two
small pieces of braai wood in hot water for 20
minutes.

Prepare a medium fire and arrange it as follows:

Move the coals to the sides of the kettle braai,
leaving an empty space in the middle. Place
the soaked wood directly on the coals to give
off smoke. "Sit" the chicken over the open can
of beer, so that the drumsticks reach down to
the bottom of the can and the bird sits upright.

Position the chicken on top of the grid over the
middle section. Cover with the lid. Open the
top vent about a third of the way. Cook, without
opening the lid for 40 minutes.

After 40 minutes turn the bird to face away from
you and cook for another 15-20 minutes until
the juices in the thickest part of the thigh run
clear when pierced with a sharp pointed knife.

Protect your hands with two wads of paper
towels and lift the bird together with the can
onto a wooden carving board. Cover lightly with
foil or greaseproof paper and rest for 10 minutes
before carving. Discard the can.

Delicious with grilled mushrooms, hot garlic
bread and a tossed salad. Dress the salad with
our Herb Salad Dressing.

VARIATION
*Baste with 1/2 cup (125 ml) of one of our Marinades
during the last 20 minutes.*

CHEF'S TIP
*The beer can be replaced with gingerbeer for a
alcohol-free variation.*

BEER BRINED PORK CHOPS WITH STICKY MARINADE

SERVES 6

2 cups (500 ml) cold tap water
1 x 340 ml bottle dark lager beer (stout)
1/4 cup (60 ml) coarse salt
6 T (90 ml) dark brown sugar
1 cup ice cubes
6-8 x 2 cm thick bone-in pork chops (loin)
1/4 cup (60 ml) olive oil
1 cup (250 ml) Ina Paarman's Sticky
   Marinade

Brining the chops beforehand makes them moist and succulent.

Combine water, beer, coarse salt and brown sugar in a large measuring jug. Stir until salt and sugar dissolves. Stir in ice. Slash through the fat and place pork chops in a large resealable plastic bag. Pour beer brine over pork chops, seal bag. Refrigerate for 30 minutes or up to 1 hour, turning the bag occasionally.

Prepare braai fire (medium-high heat). Remove pork chops from beer brine and pat dry. Brush chops with a little olive oil. Braai pork chops until done, about 10 minutes per side, occasionally moving chops to cooler part of braai if burning. Brush chops with Sticky Marinade towards the end of the cooking time. Transfer chops to a platter, cover with foil until ready to serve.

VARIATION

FOR CHICKEN BREASTS *Use 8 chicken breasts and butterfly them. Replace the beer with orange or apple juice. Baste with Lemon Marinade.*

32

CHICKEN SOSATIES WITH PEACHES AND ONION

MAKES 12 SOSATIES

250 g dried peaches, cut in half
1 x 200 ml Ina Paarman's Tikka Curry
    Coat & Cook Sauce
1/2 cup (125 ml) coconut milk or fresh
    cream
6 chicken breasts, cut into cubes
    2 cm x 2 cm
2 onions (see *Chef's Tip*)
Ina Paarman's Garlic & Herb Seasoning
sosatie sticks

Pour boiling water over the peaches and leave to stand for 10 minutes. Drain off the water and cover the peaches with clingfilm. In a medium bowl mix the Tikka Curry sauce with the coconut milk or cream. Add the chicken cubes and marinate overnight in this mixture. The next day skewer the chicken cubes onto sosatie sticks, alternating with peaches and onions. Season very lightly with Garlic and Herb seasoning. Braai or grill slowly while turning. Baste with the remaining Sauce. Bring any leftover Sauce to a fast boil and serve with the sosaties.

CHEF'S TIP

Onions: Slice from top to bottom into quarters and separate into "leaves". This is the easiest way to skewer onions.

Basting: Pour sauce into a plastic squeeze bottle with a reasonable size opening. This is better than using a brush, which may remove the tasty brown bits on the sosaties.

These delicious sosaties can also be made with cubed leg of lamb or pork fillets.

BUTTERFLIED LEMON CHICKEN

SERVES 4-6

1 large fresh free-range chicken
1 t (5 ml) Ina Paarman's Lemon & Black
**   Pepper Seasoning**
1 x 500 ml Ina Paarman's Lemon
**   Marinade**
1 large zip-lock bag

Place the chicken, breast down, on a cutting board. Use a very sharp knife or strong pair of kitchen scissors to cut along both sides of the backbone. Remove the backbone. Spread the carcass flat, breast side up. Make 3 deep slashes right down to the bone in the thighs and breasts.

Place the chicken inside a zip-lock plastic bag, add 1 cup of Lemon Marinade.

Squeeze out the air and seal the bag. Leave at room temperature for 2 hours or overnight in the fridge.

Remove chicken from the bag, discard the bag and used Marinade, and place chicken into a micro proof dish, breast up. DO NOT COVER.

Microwave open on 65% power for 20-23 minutes. Can be pre-prepared up to a day before, at this stage.

Braai, breast up, over a medium fire until beginning to brown. Then baste with fresh Marinade from the bottle. Turn and baste regularly until nicely browned all round.

Delicious with grilled polenta wedges brushed with olive oil and a well dressed salad.

The very best way to braai a whole chicken to perfection. Follow our three easy steps: Marinade, Microwave and then Braai.

LAMB AND VEGETABLE POTJIE

SERVES 6

2 kg lamb knuckles cut into 3 cm pieces
1 x 200 ml Ina Paarman's Sun-dried
    Tomato Coat & Cook Sauce
3 onions, chopped
3 T (45 ml) canola or olive oil
2 cups (500 ml) water or white wine
3 t (15 ml) Ina Paarman's Chicken Stock
    Powder
500 g baby potatoes, cut in half
4 cloves garlic, cut into slivers
    lengthways
6 large carrots, cut into thin rings
2 red bell peppers, seeded and thickly
    sliced
1 eggplant, cut into cubes
1/2 cup (125 ml) chopped parsley
1 punnet (250 g) brown mushrooms
4 T (60 ml) garlic and herb butter (see
    Chef's Tip below)
Ina Paarman's Seasoned Sea Salt

Coat the lamb knuckles with the Sun-dried Tomato sauce and leave at room temperature for 1 hour. The sauce will help to tenderise the meat. Brown the onions in the oil. Add meat, sauce and the water or wine. Add the stock powder. Stir well and allow to simmer for 1 1/2 hours. Layer the vegetables in order as given on top of the meat, seasoning each layer. Place pats of garlic and herb butter on top of the mushrooms (stem side up) season. Cook slowly without stirring for 35-45 minutes.

CHEF'S TIP
Make your own garlic butter with a lovely herb flavour: Mix 4 T (60 ml) of soft butter with 1 t (5 ml) of Ina Paarman's Garlic and Herb Seasoning.

We cooked this potjie in a clay oven and it worked brilliantly – you can do it in the usual way over a fire, but remember to heap hot coals onto the lid from time to time.

35

BRAAIED BABY CHICKENS WITH CREAMY PREGO SAUCE

SERVES 6

3 small (800 g) chickens or 6 quails
3 t (15 ml) Ina Paarman's Chilli and Garlic
    Seasoning
3 T (45 ml) butter, softened
1 t (5 ml) Ina Paarman's Garlic and Herb
    Seasoning
1 T (15 ml) lemon juice
1 t (5 ml) chicken stock powder
olive oil
1 x 200 g Ina Paarman's Ready to Serve
    Tomato and Chilli Sauce
1/2 cup (125 ml) regular or fat reduced
    cream
sosatie sticks

To butterfly the birds, place on a board, breast-side down. Using a sharp knife or kitchen scissors, cut along both sides of the backbone and remove. Turn chickens over, bend the cut ribs outwards and press down firmly on the breast bone with the palm of your hand.

Season the birds with Chilli and Garlic seasoning. Mix together the butter, Garlic and Herb seasoning, lemon juice and chicken stock powder. Divide into three. Loosen the skin carefully over the breasts and push the mixture in evenly under the skin and over the breast to ensure it remains moist.

Skewer the birds with wooden sosatie sticks through the thighs and wings to keep them flat. Brush with olive oil. Can be prepared to this point in advance and stored in the refrigerator.

When you are ready to braai, place the birds over the coals, skin side down and turn when lightly browned. Continue turning regularly and braai for about 40 minutes.

To make the Prego sauce, mix the Tomato and Chilli sauce with the cream, warm and serve on the side.

VARIATION
Our Peri-Peri Coat & Cook Sauce can be used instead of the Tomato and Chilli Ready to Serve Sauce.

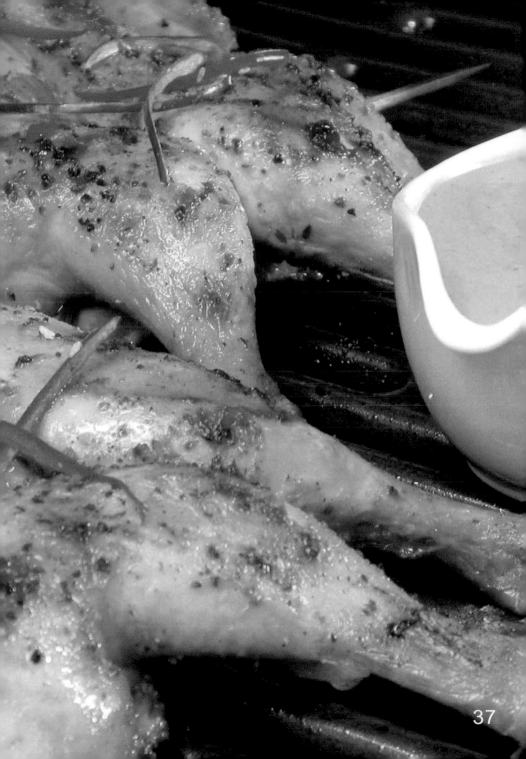

37

CURRIED CHICKEN POTJIE WITH BANANA

SERVES 6-8

8-10 chicken thighs
2 T (30 ml) flour
1 T (15 ml) medium curry powder
3 T (45 ml) canola or sunflower oil
2 t (10 ml) Ina Paarman's Chilli and Garlic
   Seasoning
2 large onions, sliced
2 large carrots, sliced
1½ cups (375 ml) long grain rice
1 x 400 g chopped tinned tomatoes
6 bananas
1 x 200 ml Ina Paarman's Tikka Curry
   Coat & Cook Sauce
2 cups (500 ml) hot water
1 T (15 ml) Ina Paarman's Chicken Stock
   Powder
1 cup (250 ml) coconut milk or regular
   or fat reduced cream
fresh coriander (optional)

Remove excess fat from thighs and dust with a mixture of flour and curry powder. Warm the potjie until hot, before adding the oil. Coat the base by tilting the pot. Add the chicken pieces in 2 batches and brown. Spoon out on a plate and season with Chilli and Garlic seasoning. When all the chicken pieces have been browned, add the onions and carrots to the remaining oil in the potjie and stir-fry until soft and aromatic. Spoon out onto a separate plate.

Now start layering the potjie. Place half the chicken pieces back in the pot, sprinkle half of the raw rice over. Add half of the vegetables and half of the tinned tomatoes. Cover with 3 sliced bananas. Repeat the layers once more. In a separate jug or bowl mix together Tikka Curry sauce, hot water, chicken stock powder and coconut milk. Pour down the side of the pot. Cover with a tight fitting lid and cook slowly over moderate coals for 1½ hours. Just before serving, top with plenty of fresh coriander leaves stripped from the bigger stems.

CHEF'S TIP
Also excellent done in the oven as a casserole. Bake in a deep casserole or ovenproof saucepan with a lid at 180°C for 1½ hours.

TO SERVE *Delicious with freshly made sambal salads of apple and tomato.*

APPLE SAMBAL
2 red skinned apples, grated
2 T (30 ml) lemon juice
¼ cup (60 ml) seedless raisins
½ t (2,5 ml) Ina Paarman's Lemon and Black
   Pepper Seasoning
Mix all ingredients together.

TOMATO SAMBAL
2 ripe tomatoes, finely diced
1 small onion, finely chopped
¼ cup (60 ml) fresh coriander
1 t (5 ml) Ina Paarman's Garlic and Herb
   Seasoning
Mix all ingredients together.

THE EDITORIAL STAFF OF *CARAVAN & OUTDOOR MAGAZINE* TESTED THIS RECIPE. THEY COMMENTED AS FOLLOWS:

"More than a palatable potjie, this dish is tasty in the extreme and will add real zing to your coal- or gas-cooking repertoire. Succulent, creamy and with a good curry kick, your family will rest replete after this meal. Contented. Sated."

BRAAIED LEG OF LAMB

SERVES 6-8

TENDERISING

1 leg of lamb, boned and opened
   butterfly-style (ask the butcher to
   "vlek" the meat so that it is not
   thicker than 3 cm in any one area)
1/2 cup (125 ml) buttermilk

Coat the leg with buttermilk and leave
   covered in a glass dish in the fridge
   overnight. Buttermilk is a wonderful
   tenderizing agent. It will not draw out
juices, nor will it alter the flavour of the
meat in any way. The next day, remove
meat and dry carefully with paper towel.

SPIKING WITH FLAVOUR

4 garlic cloves, cut into long slivers
3 rosemary twigs, cut into 2 cm lengths
10 black olives, pipped and halved

Pierce deep holes all over the lamb with
a sharp cook's knife. Lard the lamb by
   pushing a garlic sliver, rosemary snip
   and half an olive into each hole.

SEASONING

2 t (10 ml) Ina Paarman's Rosemary and
   Olive Seasoning
2 T (30 ml) olive oil

Season the meat all over and rub with olive oil.

BASTING

1 x 200 ml Ina Paarman's Olive Oil and Rosemary
   Coat & Cook Sauce or 1 cup (250 ml) Ina
   Paarman's Barbeque Marinade
olive oil

Place the meat on a hot griddle pan over the
fire in a clay oven or kettle braai, meaty side
down.

Cook for about 15 minutes until nicely browned.
Turn with a pair of tongs. Baste the cooked
side with Olive Oil and Rosemary Sauce. When
other side is nicely browned, turn and baste
with Sauce. Continue turning and basting. Use
a meat thermometer to test when done. Don't
overcook meat; it must still be slightly pink and
juicy. Cooking time varies from 45-60 minutes,
depending on thickness of joint and intensity
of heat. Rest for 10 minutes before carving.
Bring any remaining sauce with about 2-3 T
(30-45 ml) of olive oil to the boil and serve on
the side. Carve meat into thin slices and serve
on hot plates. Delicious with apricot mustard
fruits.

APRICOT MUSTARD FRUITS

MAKES ABOUT 4 CUPS

500 g dried apricots
2 t (10 ml) hot English mustard powder
2 T (30 ml) mustard seeds
1/4 cup (60 ml) water
1 cup (250 ml) cider vinegar
2 cups (400 g) white sugar
1 t (5 ml) Ina Paarman's Seasoned
   Sea Salt

Cover the apricots with hot water and hydrate
for 20 minutes. Soak the mustard powder and
seeds in 1/4 cup of cold water (for at least 10
minutes). Reserve 1 1/2 cups (375 ml) of the
apricot's soaking water and drain away the rest.

Place the apricot soak water, soaked mustard,
cider vinegar, sugar and seasoning in a medium
size saucepan. Stir over medium heat until the
sugar has dissolved. Boil fast, without a lid for
5 minutes. Add soaked apricots and simmer for
about 10 minutes until the fruit is tender.

Spoon hot into clean sterilized jars and cap.
Can be served straight away or stored in a cool
dark cupboard.

Boning a leg of lamb and opening it butterfly-style has many advantages when braaing over an open fire on a griddle pan. I love using a pot bellied stove or a pizza oven. Try this method for a fillet of venison – outstanding !

Illustrated on front cover. The problem with cooking chops on the braai is that the meat tends to overcook before the fat is crispy. This is a brilliant method of cooking chops to perfection.

SKEWERED LAMB CHOPS

SERVES 4

8-10 lamb loin chops
Ina Paarman's Rosemary and Olive Seasoning
Ina Paarman's Barbeque Marinade
sosatie sticks

Slash once or twice through the fat on the side of the chops. Season lightly with Rosemary and Olive Seasoning. Thread 4-6 chops onto a sosatie stick through the meaty eye of each chop, keeping the fatty sides lined up. Push another sosatie stick through, 1 cm away from the first one, to stabilize the meat.

Braai, with the fat-side down, over medium heat until crisp, then turn and cook the other side. Remove the chops from the sticks and lay them flat on the braai grid. Brush generously and regularly with the marinade while turning. Cook until nicely browned on the outside but still juicy inside. Use any left-over marinade to baste the chops while they are cooking.

Delicious served with tomato and onion braai sandwiches.

TOMATO AND ONION BRAAI SANDWICHES

1 small French loaf
1 x 125 g Ina Paarman's Basil Pesto
2 large ripe tomatoes, sliced
Ina Paarman's Green Onion Seasoning
2 large onions, sliced
olive oil
sosatie sticks

Slice the bread into round slices and spread one side with Basil Pesto. Place a slice of tomato seasoned with Green Onion Seasoning and a slice of onion on half of the bread slices, cover with the remaining bread slices, pesto side inside. Brush the outsides of the sandwiches with a little olive oil and secure each with a sosatie stick through the centre. Toast on the braai until golden.
VARIATION *Add a slice of mozzarella cheese to each sandwich.*

DELUXE BOEREWORS SALAD ROLLS WITH BASIL PESTO

500 g good quality boerewors
1 French loaf
olive oil
1 punnet of watercress or rocket
2 very ripe tomatoes, sliced
Ina Paarman's Green Onion Seasoning
1 wheel of feta cheese cut into thin strips
1 onion, very finely sliced and pushed
    out into rings
1 x 125 g Ina Paarman's Basil Pesto

*Let's give boerewors rolls a bit
of a face lift with some fresh
salad ingredients and crispy
French bread – a step up from
the usual soft rolls and chutney.*

Braai the boerewors in one or two straight lengths until done to your preference. Towards the end of the cooking time, put the whole unsliced French loaf on the braai and toast the outside. Remove French loaf from braai and slice lengthways, but not right through. Remove the soft interior of the bread and brush the inside with olive oil. Line the bread with green leaves and sliced tomatoes seasoned with Green Onion seasoning. Top with feta strips. Lay the sausage along the length of the bread. Add onion rings. Snip the corner of the Basil Pesto doypack and squeeze generously over the filling.

Cut into lengths for serving. Delicious with ice cold home-made lemonade (see page 17).

VARIATION *Drizzle Ina Paarman's Ready to Serve Steak and Burger Sauce over the boerewors instead of the Basil Pesto.*

43

WHOLE FILLET OVER THE COALS WITH FOUR SAUCES

SERVES 4-6

In testing this recipe we used fillets of beef, venison and ostrich. All of these worked brilliantly.

1,5-2 kg beef, venison or ostrich fillet, double over the thin tail end and tie with string
1 T (15 ml) Ina Paarman's Garlic Pepper Seasoning
1 t (5 ml) Ina Paarman's Beef Stock Powder
4 T (60 ml) olive oil

Mix the seasoning and stock powder. Sprinkle over and pat firmly into the meat. Drizzle with olive oil and turn the meat a few times to coat it thoroughly. Leave to rest at room temperature for 15 minutes.

BEST BRAAI GUIDE

1. SMOKE BOMB
Soak 1 cup of aromatic wood chips (available at supermarkets or hardware stores) in warm water for at least 30 minutes. Drain and roll in a 40 cm length of foil to form a sausage shape. Snip the foil at 5 cm intervals. This smoke bomb can be placed on the grid or directly on the coals, while the meat cooks to help impart a more intense smoke flavour.

2. FIRE
Prepare a two-level fire: One half of your kettle braai will have the coals heaped on top of each other and on the other side you will have a single layer of coals.

3. METHOD
Brown the meat all round over the heaped up coals. Turn it with tongs and don't close the lid. When the meat has been browned all round, move it over to the cooler side of the braai. Place the smoke bomb on the fire.

Close the lid and open the top vent 2/3 of the way. Position the vent opposite the side where you have your smoke bomb, so that the smoke is drawn across the meat and not straight up and out.

Calculate cooking time at about 15 minutes per 500 g. I firmly believe that the most accurate method is to insert a meat thermometer into the thickest part of the meat. Medium-rare will register 70-71°C.

NB. DO NOT OPEN THE LID too often or much of the smoke will be lost!

4. SAUCES
PEPPER SAUCE – 1 x 200 ml Ina Paarman's Ready to Serve Pepper Sauce. Thin down with a little strong beef stock and warm before serving.

HOT PREGO SAUCE – 1 x 200 ml Ina Paarman's Peri-Peri Coat & Cook Sauce mixed with 1/2 cup (125 ml) fat reduced cream.
Serve warm or at room temperature.

MEXICAN SAUCE – 1 x 200 ml Ina Paarman's Ready to Serve Tomato and Chilli Sauce mixed and garnished with 3 T (45 ml) snipped fresh coriander leaves. Serve at room temperature.

MUSHROOM SAUCE – 1 x 200 ml Ina Paarman's Ready to Serve Mushroom Sauce. Thin down with a little milk and warm before serving.

5. HOW TO SERVE
When the internal temperature of the meat is to your preference remove it from the fire and leave to stand, covered with foil, for 10 minutes to settle the juices before carving.

CHEF'S TIP *Pre-seasoning and oiling the fillet and leaving the meat out at room temperature gave superb results.*

LEMON GLAZED LEG OF PORK ON THE BRAAI

SERVES 10-12

1 small leg of pork ± 3,5 kg (ask the butcher to score the skin in a diamond pattern)
Ina Paarman's Lemon and Black Pepper Seasoning
olive oil
1 cup (250 ml) Ina Paarman's Lemon Marinade

Slice through the skin of the leg on the sides and remove the skin on top of the leg, cut quite close to the skin with a small, sharp pointed knife so that you don't remove the fat from the leg. Prick the skin all over and put the skin open and unwrapped in the fridge on a piece of kitchen paper to dry it out. This gives extra crispness to the crackling.

Rub the meat all over with Lemon and Black Pepper Seasoning first and then with olive oil. Cover and leave in the fridge overnight. Bring to room temperature before cooking.

Light the gas braai or prepare a slow fire in your kettle braai. Keep some back-up briquettes to add to the fire as the leg will cook slowly for ± 3 hours depending on size. Place the meat on the grid and cook slowly. Regularly baste the leg with Lemon Marinade during the last hour of cooking. **DO NOT TURN THE MEAT.** Keep basting it with marinade every 20 minutes until all the sauce has been used. Towards the end of the cooking time remove the skin from the fridge. Take the meat off the braai and leave to rest covered for 15 minutes before carving.

Turn up the gas or add more coals to the fire. Cut the skin into strips and rub with Lemon and Black Pepper Seasoning and olive oil. Start cooking it on the skin side first until crisp and bubbly. Now cook the fat side until the fat is crispy. Carve the rested leg into neat slices. Serve each guest with a few meat slices and a piece of crispy crackling on the side. Quince purèe or apple sauce are both excellent with pork.

We served the leg with cheesy polenta tartlets topped with basil pesto and baby tomatoes (see page 10). A huge green salad topped with all your favourite trimmings will always be a hit.

CHEF'S TIP
If you prefer to use a conventional oven, set the oven on 170°C and roast for ±3 hours.

This is the ultimate leg of pork! Wonderfully glamorous to entertain with, far more economical than the usual steak and chops and lean and healthy to boot! The lemon baste complements pork particularly well. Serve with a sweetish quince or apple sauce on the side.

SKEWERED CHIPOLATAS WITH DEVILS ON HORSEBACK

SERVES 8-10

250 g rindless streaky bacon
250 g de-pipped prunes
500 g chipolata sausages
1 x 200 ml Ina Paarman's Ready to Serve
    Mustard Sauce
sosatie sticks

Cut each bacon strip in half across the width and roll one prune in a piece of bacon. Thread the wrapped prunes and chipolata sausages onto sosatie sticks. Braai slowly or cook in the oven at 200°C for ± 25 minutes. Place on a flat serving dish and serve with Mustard Sauce on the side to spoon over or dip into.

VARIATION

Use our Honey and Soy Coat & Cook Sauce as a dip.

47

BRAAIED VEGETABLE MEDLEY

ON THE SIDE

I often bake vegetables ahead of time. Serve them at room temperature or just re-heat them on the braai fire, in the same oven pan in which they were baked.

BLAST BAKED VEGETABLES

SERVES 8

Ina Paarman's Rosemary and Olive Seasoning
2 large eggplants, sliced lengthways
6 baby marrows
2 red bell peppers, seeded and quartered lengthways
2 yellow bell peppers, seeded and quartered lengthways
6 black mushrooms
Ina Paarman's Lemon and Black Pepper Seasoning
1 cup (250 ml) Ina Paarman's Herb Salad Dressing

Preheat the oven to 250°C.

Lightly season the eggplant with Rosemary and Olive seasoning and leave in a colander for 20 minutes.

Slice all the vegetables on the diagonal into strips. Season the marrows and peppers with Rosemary and Olive seasoning.

Season the mushrooms with Lemon and Black Pepper seasoning. Drizzle Herb Salad dressing over all the vegetables to coat and spread out onto two oven-roasting pans in single layers.

Roast for about 30-40 minutes, until the vegetables are browning on the edges.

CARAMELISED PEARL ONIONS IN TOMATO AND CHILLI SAUCE

SERVES 6-8

750 g pearl (baby) onions
2 T (30 ml) olive oil
2 T (30 ml) sugar
3 T (45 ml) balsamic vinegar
Ina Paarman's Green Onion or Lemon
    and Black Pepper Seasoning
1/2 cup (125 ml) water
1 x 200 ml Ready to Serve Tomato and
    Chilli Sauce
2 spring onions, finely sliced

To skin the onions, first top and tail them, then cover with boiling water. Leave for 3-5 minutes. Drain and rinse under cold water. Slip off the skins.

Warm the oil in a wide frying pan and add the onions. Shake the pan to roll and brown them, then add sugar, balsamic vinegar and seasoning. Simmer open over medium heat until almost all the vinegar has evaporated. Add water and cover with a tight fitting lid. Simmer slowly for 10-12 minutes or until onions are done. Remove pan from the heat and add the Tomato and Chilli sauce. Do not boil. Leave to cool down.

Serve at room temperature, garnished with finely sliced spring onions.

I just love this method of cooking onions by rolling them in a hot frying pan. The balsamic vinegar gives excellent flavour depth. Delicious with both braaied and cold meats.

51

BRAAIED VEGETABLE MEDLEY

SERVES 4-6

CORN ON THE COB (MIELIES)

4-6 whole mielies with leaves
3 T (45 ml) garlic and herb butter (see *Chef's Tip* on page 63)
2 t (10 ml) Ina Paarman's Green Onion Seasoning

Gently peel back the green outer leaves and remove the silk threads on each mielie. Spread with garlic and herb butter and season with Green Onion seasoning. Bring the green leaves back up to cover and secure in place with string. Braai for 20-30 minutes.

MUSHROOMS

4-6 big brown mushrooms
1 T (15 ml) butter
1 T (15 ml) olive oil
zest of one lemon
1 cup (250 ml) fresh white breadcrumbs
2 t (10 ml) Ina Paarman's Garlic Pepper Seasoning

Melt the butter and mix together with the olive oil, lemon zest, breadcrumbs and Garlic Pepper seasoning. Spoon a generous helping into each mushroom and press to set firmly. Braai, stem side up, for 20-30 minutes.

VEGETABLE SKEWERS

2 red bell peppers, seeded and sliced
1 eggplant, sliced
2 onions
Ina Paarman's Herb Salad Dressing
Ina Paarman's Garlic and Herb Seasoning

Cut the peppers and eggplant slices into triangular shapes. Cut the onions into wedges. Thread vegetables onto metal skewers, alternating peppers, eggplant and onion. Brush generously with Herb salad dressing and season. Braai for 20-30 minutes, turning regularly and basting with Herb dressing.

GRILLED BABY LEEKS WITH GREEN ONION YOGHURT SAUCE

SERVES 4

2 punnets baby leeks, trim root end and
    neaten tops
1 T (15 ml) olive oil
Ina Paarman's Green Onion Seasoning
kebab sticks

Rinse the leeks in a big bowl of water
to remove any sand trapped in the
leaves. Thread 2 kebab sticks through
every 6 leeks to form a "mat". Brush
with oil on both sides. Grill the leeks
on a ribbed griddle pan or over a
medium-hot fire turning once, until
tender and streaked with light grill
marks, 5 to 7 minutes. Remove the
sticks and transfer the grilled leeks to
a platter. Season to taste. Serve warm
or at room temperature with the yoghurt
sauce.

GREEN ONION YOGHURT SAUCE
1 x 250 g tub smooth cottage cheese
3/4 cup (180ml) plain yoghurt
1/4 cup (60 ml) finely sliced spring onions
1 t (5 ml) Ina Paarman's Green Onion
    Seasoning
Mix all the ingredients for the sauce
together. Serve in a bowl on the side.

VARIATION *Asparagus works well prepared
the same way.*

*Use baby leeks no thicker
than 1 cm because mature
leeks are too tough and
will burn on the surface
before they cook through.*

53

OVEN ROAST TOMATO SALAD WITH ROAST GARLIC AND CRUSHED OLIVES

SERVES 4

**350 g baby tomatoes cut lengthways
through the middle and quartered
Ina Paarman's Seasoned Sea Salt
2 t (10 ml) sugar
20 cloves of garlic, peeled
2 T (30 ml) olive oil
1/2 cup (125 ml) calamata olives
1/4 cup (60 ml) Ina Paarman's Italian
Balsamic or Greek Lemon Vinaigrette
rocket leaves and butter lettuce**

Preheat the oven to 170°C.

Arrange tomatoes cut side up on a baking sheet, season and sprinkle with sugar.

Season garlic and toss with olive oil in a separate small ovenproof dish.

Roast tomatoes and garlic at the same time. The garlic will be ready after 35 minutes, leave the tomatoes in for another 30 minutes, until they are less plump. Can be prepared up to this stage a day ahead and refrigerated in a covered container.

Smash the olives in a plastic bag with the smooth side of a meat mallet. Arrange the tomato and garlic on a mixture of the leaves, add the olives and dress the salad. Excellent with braaied chicken, a selection of cheeses and crusty bread.

*The intense flavours in this
salad are excellent.*

SWEET PEPPER SALAD

SERVES 8

3 red bell peppers
3 yellow bell peppers
2 t (10 ml) Ina Paarman's Lemon and
 Black Pepper Seasoning
1/2 cup (125 ml) Ina Paarman's Greek
 Lemon Vinaigrette
grated rind of one lemon

Preheat the oven to 250°C.

Bake the peppers on a rack over a roasting pan for about 20-25 minutes until blistered and blackening on the outside.

Place them in a glass mixing bowl and cover tightly with clingfilm – leave to sweat and cool down.

In the process the skin will loosen itself from the flesh. Pull off the blistered skin (it does not matter if a bit remains here and there). Remove the stems and seeds. Cut the peppers lengthways into 1-2 cm strips. Season, arrange on a platter and add dressing. Sprinkle with grated lemon rind. Serve at room temperature. Keeps very well in the fridge for up to 3 days if kept covered.

55

 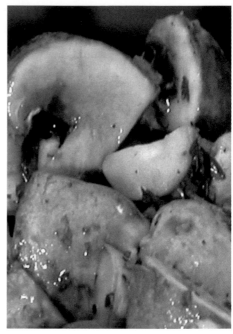

MINTED BEETROOT SALAD WITH FETA

SERVES 6-8

6 medium beetroots, baked or boiled
1-2 t (5–10 ml) Ina Paarman's Lemon and
    Black Pepper Seasoning
1/4 cup (60 ml) Ina Paarman's Honey
    Mustard Dressing
1 T (15 ml) whole grain mustard
1 cup (250 ml) fresh mint, washed and
    roughly chopped
2-3 wheels of plain feta cheese

Skin the cooked beetroot and cut into small wedges (± 8 each). Season generously with Lemon and Black Pepper seasoning and toss, while still warm, with dressing and mustard. Just before serving, top the salad with mint and crumbled feta.

MARINATED MUSHROOMS WITH GARLIC

SERVES 6

1 x punnet (250 g) portobellini mushrooms
1 x punnet (250 g) button mushrooms
1 cup (250 ml) water
1/2 cup (125 ml) white vinegar
10 cloves of garlic, sliced into long slivers
handful fresh parsley, chopped
1 t (5 ml) Ina Paarman's Garlic Pepper Seasoning
1 cup (250 ml) Ina Paarman's Italian Balsamic
    Vinaigrette

Wipe and quarter the mushrooms. Bring water and vinegar to the boil. Add mushrooms and cook for 30 seconds only, with the lid on. Drain immediately. Toss with garlic, parsley, seasoning and dressing to coat well. Keep in a sealed container in the fridge. Serve at room temperature.

SALAD OF BUTTERNUT, OLIVE, ROCKET AND TOMATO

SERVES 6

1 medium size butternut
1/4 cup (60 ml) olive oil
Ina Paarman's Rosemary and Olive
  Seasoning
250 g baby tomatoes, halved
1/2 cup (125 ml) black olives, drained,
  pipped and sliced in half through the
  middle
1/4 cup (60 ml) Ina Paarman's Greek
  Lemon Vinaigrette
2 handfuls of rocket leaves
1/4 cup (60 ml) pumpkin seeds, lightly
  toasted in a dry frying pan

Preheat the oven to 200°C.

Peel the butternut, remove seeds, and cut into 2 cm x 2 cm cubes. Place in a shallow ovenproof dish and toss lightly with olive oil. Season with Rosemary and Olive seasoning and roast for about 35 minutes, until tender and lightly browned. Transfer the butternut cubes to a large bowl and add the tomatoes and olives. Add Lemon Vinaigrette and toss gently. Season to taste. Place salad on a bed of rocket leaves on individual plates and scatter with toasted pumpkin seeds.

Mediterranean potatoes are really good to use in this salad, otherwise use red potatoes or any potato variety recommended for chips.

PESTO POTATO SALAD WITH GREEN BEANS

SERVES 6-8

1 kg potatoes, unpeeled
250 g green beans, trimmed and cut into
  2 cm lengths on the diagonal
1/4 cup (60 ml) Ina Paarman's Basil Pesto
1 t (5 ml) Ina Paarman's Green Onion
  Seasoning
1/4 cup (60 ml) finely snipped spring
  onions
2 T (30 ml) olive oil

Steam the potatoes until tender. Leave to cool. Steam the beans until just tender but still bright green. Toss beans with pesto while still warm.

Skin and cut potatoes into small wedges. Season with Green Onion Seasoning. Gently toss with the dressed green beans, spring onions and olive oil. Serve at room temperature.

VARIATION
Also lovely served hot as a vegetable accompaniment to braaied chicken.

MUSTARD PICKLED VEGETABLES

SERVES 12 AS A SIDE DISH

6 baby marrows, quartered lengthways
12 baby corn, halved lengthways
1 yellow bell pepper, seeded and cut into strips
2 red bell peppers, seeded and cut into strips
1 chilli, finely sliced
3 large carrots, cut into fine julienne strips
3 cloves garlic, cut into slivers

PICKLING LIQUID
1 T (15 ml) hot English mustard powder
3 T (45 ml) cold water
1 cup (250 ml) wine vinegar or cider vinegar
1 cup (250 ml) water
1 cup (250 ml) white sugar
1 T (15 ml) Ina Paarman's Seasoned Sea Salt

Mix the mustard powder and cold water and leave to stand for 10 minutes. Bring the vinegar, water and sugar to a rapid boil. Mix in the mustard and seasoned sea salt. Add the vegetables and boil for 3 minutes. Pack into a clean glass container and fill up with boiling hot pickling liquid. Seal immediately. These pickled vegetables are best after standing overnight. Keeps refrigerated for 2 weeks.

One of our best long-life fridge salads.

59

The toasted bread makes this salad a hit, even with those non-salad eaters.

TUSCAN SALAD

SERVES 4

¹/2 ciabatta (Italian bread)
500 g ripe baby tomatoes
Ina Paarman's Green Onion Seasoning
¹/2 cup (125 ml) Ina Paarman's Italian
   Balsamic Vinaigrette
a handful fresh basil leaves
1 punnet rocket leaves

Preheat the oven to 240°C.

Slice the bread and roughly tear the slices into small pieces and place on a baking tray. Bake in the oven for about 5-10 minutes until dry and toasted on the outside. Place in a bowl.

Cut 12 of the tomatoes in half through the middle, and using your hands, squeeze them over the toasted bread. Season with Green Onion seasoning. Pour the dressing over the toasted bread mixture and toss.

Slice remaining tomatoes lengthways and add, with the basil and rocket, to the bread mixture.

CAPE STYLE WHOLE WHEAT BREAD

MAKES 1 LARGE LOAF

4 cups (480 g) whole wheat flour
1 cup (120 g) white bread flour
1 x 10 g packet instant dry yeast
1 T (15 ml) brown sugar
4 blocks of Weet-Bix, finely crushed
2 t (10 ml) salt
1/4 cup (60 ml) sesame seeds or toasted
    sunflower seeds
2 cups (500 ml) lukewarm water
2 cups (500 ml) buttermilk at room
    temperature
2 T (30 ml) canola or grapeseed oil
some extra seeds to sprinkle over the top

Oil or butter a 28 cm x 11 cm bread pan. Line the base with a strip of baking or buttered greaseproof paper.

Measure the two kinds of flour into a large, sturdy mixing bowl. Add the yeast and sugar. Crush the Weet-Bix in a plastic bag with a meat mallet or small saucepan and add to the flour. Add the salt and seeds and stir to blend. Make a hollow in the flour and add the lukewarm water, buttermilk and oil. Stir with a strong wooden spoon until the mixture is very well blended. Add a little more water if the mixture is too heavy to stir. Spoon the bread mixture into the prepared pan. Sprinkle with some extra seeds. Leave in a warm spot (see *Chef's Tip*) until the bread has nearly risen to the top of the pan.

Halfway through the rising time preheat the oven to 200°C.

Bake for 1 hour. Remove the bread from the pan 5-10 minutes before the time is up and continue baking without the pan for the final 5-10 minutes to crisp the bottom crust.

CHEF'S TIP

This is the method we use to create the warm humid atmosphere that yeast loves. Place a roasting pan half filled with warm water in a black bin liner. Put a rack or trivet over the roasting pan and then put the pan with bread mixture on top of the rack. Tie the bag closed to keep the heat in. The bread will take about 35-55 minutes to rise. Don't be in too much of a hurry. Slower is better.

OVERNIGHT PROOFING

The prepared mixture, in the mixing bowl (covered with clingfilm), can also be put in the fridge to rise slowly overnight. The next day or a few hours later, give the risen bread a good stir, spoon into the pan and leave to rise for a second time in a warm spot until it has nearly risen to the top of the pan. Bake as above.

GRILLED FLAT BREADS

SERVES 12

3 cups (360 g) bread flour
1/4 cup (40 g) mealie meal (polenta)
2 t (10 ml) Ina Paarman's Rosemary and
   Olive Seasoning
1 x 10 g packet instant dry yeast
1 1/4 cups (310 ml) lukewarm water
olive oil

Place all the dry ingredients in a mixing bowl. Add the water to the dry ingredients to make a soft dough. Knead well until the dough is smooth and silky. The dough may also be prepared very successfully in a food processor or large mixer with a dough-hook attachment. Pour a little olive oil into the bowl and coat the dough with it. Leave overnight in the fridge or, if you are in a hurry, in a warm spot to double in size.

Knead again and shape into 16-18 flat, even-sized disks (see *Chef's Tip*). Place the rounds well spaced on a floured baking sheet and leave in a warm spot until puffy (about 20 minutes). Cook the breads on the braai or directly on a griddle pan until dark brown markings appear. Flip over and grill until brown. An optional extra is to knead a few needles of fresh rosemary, sun-dried tomato quarters, sliced olives, etc. in to the dough before kneading for the first time.

The breads may also be baked in the oven at 250°C for 10-15 minutes.

CHEF'S TIP
Roll the dough out about 1 cm thick and cut into rounds with a 10 cm plain round biscuit cutter.

These bread disks are cooked directly on a braai or on a griddle pan in a clay oven. Serve them drizzled with olive oil or stuffed with sliced braaied meat or fish.

HOT CHEESE AND TOMATO PESTO BREAD

SERVES 6-8

1 French loaf
150 g of garlic and herb butter
    (see *Chef's Tip*)
1 x 125 g Ina Paarman's Sun-dried
    Tomato Pesto
150 g Emmenthaler cheese
basil leaves

Preheat the oven to 180°C.

Slice a French loaf at 2 cm intervals, but do not cut all the way through. Open each alternate gap and spread with garlic and herb butter. Spread Sun-dried Tomato Pesto between the remaining slices. Place a generous slice of cheese between bread slices spread with pesto. Wrap the bread snugly in foil and heat through for 15-20 minutes.

Serve hot, garnished with fresh basil leaves.

VARIATION
Heat through on the braai if more convenient.

CHEF'S TIP
Make your own garlic butter with a lovely herb flavour: Mix 150 g of soft butter with 2 t (10 ml) of Ina Paarman's Garlic and Herb Seasoning.

INDEX